HAUNTED CHURCHES AND GRAVEYARDS

VIC KOVACS

CRABTREE
PUBLISHING COMPANY
WWW.CRABTREEBOOKS.COM

HAUNTED OR HOAX?

Author: Vic Kovacs

Editors: Marcia Abramson, Petrice Custance

Photo research: Melissa McClellan

Cover/interior design: T.J. Choleva

Proofreader: Lorna Notsch

**Production coordinator and
  prepress technician:** Tammy McGarr

Print coordinator: Katherine Berti

Consultant: Susan Demeter-St. Clair
  Paranormal Studies & Inquiry

Written and produced for Crabtree Publishing by
BlueAppleWorks Inc.

Photographs & Illustrations
Cover illustration: T.J Choleva (background image: Anastasios Kandris/Shutterstock; front image:
Joe Prachatree/Shutterstock
Title page illustration: Joshua Avramson (background image Creaturart Images/Shutterstock.com;
front image: Jeff Thrower/Shutterstock
Shutterstock.com: © Login (page backgrounds); © Venus Kaewyoo (p. 5, 17 middle); ©
andreiuc88 (p. 5, 15 sidebar); © Hollygraphic (p. 9 bottom); © Nomad_Soul (p. 9 bottom right);
© dugdax (p. 9, 21 sidebar); © Ensuper (p. 9 middle); © Christian Hinkle (p. 10 top right); © Joseph
Becker (p. 11, 25 middle); © Basileus (p. 11, 23 sidebar); © DIIMSA Researcher (p. 12 top right); ©
David Litman (p. 12 bottom); © faestock(p. 13 middle); © lukaszsokol
(p. 13 sidebar); © cherezoff (p. 15 middle); © Aleksey Stemmer (p. 17 sidebar); © Bertl123
(p. 18 top right); © Dan Bridge (p. 19 top right); © g-stockstudio (p. 18 bottom right); © Andrey_
Kuzmin (p. 21, 23 middle); © Paolo Costa (p. 21 top right); © Asvolas (p. 21 bottom right); ©
Imagine Photographer (p. 21, 25 sidebar); © Stas Guk (p. 23 top right); © Skreidzeleu (p. 23 middle
right); © Matyas Rehak (p. 24 top right, p. 24 middle right); © Alexander Mazurkevich (p. 24
bottom); © pan_kung (p. 24 bottom middle); © Vladimir Melnik (p. 26 bottom middle); © Orhan
Cam(p. 27 bottom right); © Evgeny Haritonov (p. 27 sidebar)
Creative Commons: Chris Gunns (p. 6 top right); Keith Evans (p. 9 top right); Shahnoor Habib
Munmun (p.11 top right); Gryffindor (p. 15 top right); Ayleen Gaspar (p. 16–17 bottom); Kim
Traynor (p. 19 bottom left); Carlos Delgado (p. 18–19 bottom); Dnalor 01 (p. 22 top right, p. 22
bottom); Tessier~commonswiki (p. 22 middle right); Nikola Smolenski (p. 26–27 bottom)
Public Domain: Metropolitan Museum of Art (p. 26 left); Harvey Metcalfe (p. 29 right)
Muslianshah Masrie/Alamy Stock Photo (p. 28 bottom)
Joshua Avramson p. 4–5 bottom (background image Creaturart Images/Shutterstock.com); p.
6–7 (background image Helen Hotson/Shutterstock.com, front right image Olena Yakobchuk/
Shutterstock.com); p. 8 bottom (background image Poliphilo/Creative Commons); p. 10 bottom
(background image SNEHIT/Shutterstock.com); p. 14 bottom
(left figure Tom Wang/Shutterstock.com); p. 17 top right; p. 20–21 bottom (background image
iolya/Shutterstock.com
T.J Choleva p. 11 (background image Zack Frank/Shutterstock.com; p. 19 sidebar; p. 25
(background image Gavin J Dronfield/Shutterstock.com, front image kurhan/Shutterstock.com)
Carlyn Iverson p. 13

Library and Archives Canada Cataloguing in Publication

Kovacs, Vic, author
    Haunted churches and graveyards / Vic Kovacs.

(Haunted or hoax?)
Includes index.
Issued in print and electronic formats.
ISBN 978-0-7787-4630-0 (hardcover).--
ISBN 978-0-7787-4641-6 (softcover).--
ISBN 978-1-4271-2054-0 (HTML)

    1. Haunted cemeteries--Juvenile literature. 2. Church buildings--
Juvenile literature. 3. Ghosts--Juvenile literature. I. Title.

BF1474.3.K68 2018   j133.1'22   C2017-907786-4
                                            C2017-907787-2

Library of Congress Cataloging-in-Publication Data

CIP available at the Library of Congress

Crabtree Publishing Company
www.crabtreebooks.com   1-800-387-7650

Printed in the U.S.A./032018/BG20180202

Published in Canada
Crabtree Publishing
616 Welland Ave.
St. Catharines, Ontario
L2M 5V6

Published in the United States
Crabtree Publishing
PMB 59051
350 Fifth Avenue, 59th Floor
New York, New York 10118

Published in the United Kingdom
Crabtree Publishing
Maritime House
Basin Road North, Hove
BN41 1WR

Published in Australia
Crabtree Publishing
3 Charles Street
Coburg North
VIC, 3058

CONTENTS

OTHERWORLDLY PLACES

For most of recorded history, human beings have wondered about ghosts. Are they real? Do the spirits of the dead really return to haunt the living? If they do, why? And why are ghosts seemingly more attracted to some places than others? People often say they see ghosts and **specters** in churches and graveyards, which they connect with the spirit world and the **afterlife**.

Graveyards in particular have always been the subject of haunting stories and legends. It's easy to see why. Where is a ghost more likely to appear than in the place its **mortal** remains lie resting for eternity? For many people, walking through a creepy graveyard late at night makes them more likely to believe something seen out of the corner of their eye might be a ghost.

DID YOU KNOW?

Is there a difference between a cemetery and a graveyard? Today, the words are used to mean basically the same thing. Originally, though, there was a difference. Traditionally, graveyards were smaller and connected to a church in some way. Cemeteries were larger and not associated with a particular church.

Graveyards, and their close connection with death, make many people uncomfortable.

Are They Real?

Many people today believe in ghosts. Many others do not. These skeptics believe that supposedly **supernatural** events can be explained easily. There are even investigators who research and visit "haunted" places to try and figure out the truth! What do you think? Are hauntings just cases of people with active imaginations seeing things that aren't there? Or is there more to this world than science understands?

SPIRIT MEDIUMS

Some people claim that they can communicate with those in the afterlife directly. These people are known as spirit mediums. Some say they can be **possessed** by a spirit that speaks through them. Others say they talk to the dead using special equipment, such as a Ouija ("wee-gee") board. This board has letters and a pointer that people touch lightly. It is said that spirits guide a user's hands to spell out messages.

Some mediums have been revealed as **frauds** who use tricks to convince people they are talking to dead loved ones. Still, belief in these abilities remains.

HAUNTED RUIN OF KNOWLTON CHURCH

Knowlton Church is located in Dorset, in southwestern England. It was built in the 1100s. It stands in the center of a much older **pagan** site of worship called a henge. A henge is a round **earthwork**. Many henges have tall standing stones inside. The most famous example is Stonehenge, which is also in southwest England.

The builders likely put Knowlton Church inside the circle to help local pagans accept Christianity. They broke up standing stones that had been there for thousands of years. Some stones were used for building. Others were just buried.

Historians believe the Knowlton henge was constructed between 3000 B.C.E. and 2000 B.C.E.

By the late 1400s, the **plague** had come to Knowlton. Anyone lucky enough to survive left the village. The church still brought in people from the surrounding area until the roof collapsed, almost 300 years later. After that, it quickly became a ruin.

It is said the Knowlton ruins are haunted by the spirits of both Christians and pagans.

Den of Ghosts

Knowlton Church today is a hollowed-out ruin, but some say it still has a number of ghostly residents. There have been reports of a phantom horse and rider traveling across the area and right through the church! People have seen an eerie face peering out at them from the highest window in the church's ruined tower. A weeping woman, possibly a nun, has been seen kneeling outside the church. Whatever terrible act she's still asking forgiveness for all these years later is a secret lost to the ages. **Paranormal** investigators have studied the site. Some have reported seeing mysterious swirling mists and hearing ghostly voices. However, nothing has ever been proven.

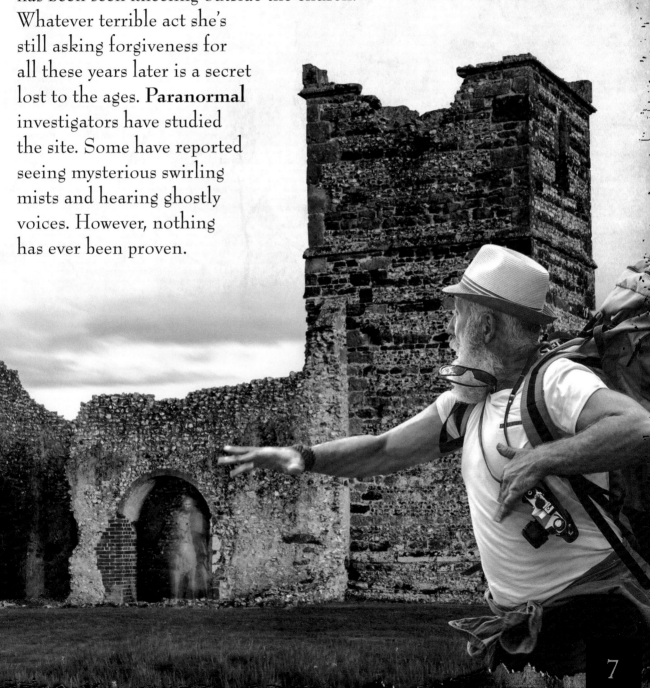

BRITAIN'S MOST HAUNTED

Pluckley is a community in the county of Kent in England. It was once listed in the *Guinness Book of Records* as the most haunted place in the entire country! One of the most famous ghosts in the area is the Red Lady. Her legend states that, in life, she was known as Lady Dering.

The Derings lived in the area for 500 years, and it's not known exactly when she died. Her ghost is said to wander the churchyard of St. Nicholas Church. It's claimed that her spirit is searching for the grave of her lost baby. The reason for her nickname is also unclear. Some believe it's because she's always seen wearing a long, flowing red dress. Others say it's because of the red rose that was placed on her coffin when she died.

According to legend, there's not only a Red Lady outside the church, but also a White Lady who haunts the inside!

But Wait, There's More!

Of course, the most haunted place in England has more than just one ghost story! Other **apparitions** that have been reported include a miller at a windmill and a monk outside a house called Greystones. People also say they still hear the screams of a worker who was crushed by a falling wall at an old brickworks.

Pluckley today has about 1,000 people and at least 15 reported ghosts. TV shows have made the village famous. So many tourists come for Halloween that police worry more about crowds than ghosts!

BORLEY CHURCH

A church in Essex County, England, may have inherited ghosts! Borley Church is near the site of Borley Rectory, which was called the most haunted house in England until it was torn down in 1944 after a fire. Since then, more paranormal activity has been reported at the church. This includes mysterious organ music, lights, and chanting, as well as a phantom nun and a ghostly monk.

LOOK AT THE EVIDENCE

Many investigators came to Borley Rectory when it was considered the most haunted house in England. One investigation by a big broadcasting company even concluded that the **phenomena** were real. In 2000, though, Louis Mayerling said he and other residents had been playing tricks. He said a piano was made to play by plucking its strings with a poker through a wall gap. He also said he walked the grounds dressed as a headless ghost. But Mayerling's book didn't rule out ghosts entirely. He said kitchen bells once rang out although no one was ringing them as part of the hoax! Some people say Mayerling's book itself is a hoax. What do you think?

GHOSTS
OF THE PAST

New Orleans, Louisiana, is a city rich with history. It is also considered one of the most haunted cities in all of the United States. Ghost tours are popular attractions for visitors, and many locals have ghost stories of their own. One of the most famous haunted landmarks in New Orleans is St. Louis **Cathedral**, one of the oldest cathedrals in the country.

The first St. Louis Cathedral was built in 1727. It has been rebuilt several times. The current building is from the 1850s.

Ghost of the Spanish Priest

The most well-known ghost said to call the cathedral home is Père Antoine. The Spanish priest arrived in New Orleans in 1744 and became pastor of the cathedral. By the time of his death in 1829, he was loved by the entire city. It's said he was buried under the church. Many people have claimed to see his ghost, especially around Christmas. Père Antoine is easy to recognize because his portrait still hangs in the church!

An alley located near the cathedral was named for Père Antoine. People often say they see him walking there early in the morning.

Hauntings of a Priestess

The St. Louis Cemetery #1 is also said to be haunted. Marie Laveau, a famous **voodoo** priestess, was laid to rest there— but she may not be resting easy. People say Laveau haunts not only the cemetery but the whole city, where she was known for good deeds, as well as powerful magic.

People still come to Marie Laveau's tomb to ask her spirit for favors. They often leave coins, flowers, and other gifts. Some claim to have seen her ghost.

ST. ANDREW'S ON THE RED

St. Andrew's on the Red is an old church just outside Winnipeg, Manitoba. It was built in the 1840s and is the oldest stone church in western Canada. Life was hard for settlers in the area. Many died of disease and were buried in the cemetery overlooking the Red River. It's said their spirits haunt St. Andrew's, including a set of glowing red eyes, a man in black, and a woman in white. Many people have nightmares for weeks after visiting St. Andrew's. Even stranger, many different visitors have reported having the same dream—unseen hands shaking the cemetery gates.

LOOK AT THE EVIDENCE

Although many people have reported ghostly experiences at St. Andrew's on the Red, are ghosts really the only possible explanation? Skeptics might say that the red eyes people claim to see could just belong to an animal, such as a stray cat. Or they could just be light reflecting off an object that's hard to see in the dark. What could some other explanations be?

11

GHOSTS SPAWNED BY HURRICANES

A hurricane is one of the most destructive events in nature. But are hurricanes also able to give rise to the unquiet dead? Some people think the answer is yes.

St. Paul's Church

Key West, Florida, has a long history of hurricanes, piracy, smuggling—and ghosts. Paranormal events have been reported all over the island. Many are associated with St. Paul's Episcopal Church and its cemetery. The church has seen many disasters, including deadly hurricanes and the Great Key West Fire of 1886. It has been rebuilt several times since the first church was built in the 1800s.

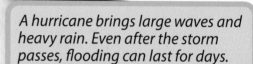

A hurricane brings large waves and heavy rain. Even after the storm passes, flooding can last for days.

The current church building was finished in 1919. It's mostly made of concrete to protect against hurricanes. The cemetery, though, is still exposed to storms.

Angry Ghosts

One of the worst occurrences at St. Paul's came in 1928. That year, a devastating hurricane swept through the area. Hurricane Okeechobee was a Category 5, the strongest level for a hurricane. The high winds and waters damaged or destroyed all the graves at St. Paul's. Bodies and bones that had been inside the graves were found everywhere, even up in treetops.

As a result, most of the ghostly activity reported at the church is actually located in the graveyard. Many believe the ghosts are angry that their remains were disturbed and not properly reburied.

KEY WEST – THE BONE ISLAND

Hurricane Okeechobee turned up another part of Key West's spooky past. Not all the bones were from the cemetery. Native peoples had long lived in the area before Europeans arrived. The custom of these Native peoples was to bury their dead on the beaches. According to legend, when the Spanish explorers arrived, they found bones everywhere. The original name of Key West in Spanish was "Cayo Hueso," which can be translated as "falling bones."

After the hurricane, the bodies in St. Paul's cemetery had to be reburied quickly because of the Florida heat.

13

Fighting Spirit

The land for St. Paul's graveyard was originally a gift to the church from the **widow** of a man named John Fleming. His last request was that the new graveyard remain his final burial place. Many storms have disturbed John Fleming's grave. One story even says his headstone is now part of the church's walls! So, perhaps anger over this is why his ghost has reportedly been spotted in the area. People have also claimed to have seen ghosts huddling around a statue of an angel. There's even supposedly a ghost of a man who fought pirates off Key West when he was alive. Apparently, he still has that fighting spirit in death, because it's claimed that he has attacked visitors to the graveyard. Locals make sure to stay away from the cemetery at night.

Were tourists really attacked at St. Paul's cemetery? Ghost tours can be scary, so perhaps their imaginations went wild.

Built on Bones

Captain Tony's is a bar in Key West that is also considered a paranormal hot spot. Its building dates to 1852, when it was the city **morgue**. That makes Captain Tony's creepy for many people right from the start. On top of that, a tree near the original building was once used for hangings. People believed anyone who harmed the tree would be cursed. So when Captain Tony's building was expanded, it was built around the tree. Eighteen pirates were hung from the tree, as well as one woman who killed her family. Many people say they have seen her ghost wearing the blue dress she died in. She's called the Lady in Blue.

Locals say that the Lady in Blue has plenty of ghostly company. In the 1980s, workers found human bones under the bar during a renovation. There was even a grave marker with the name "Elvira." Some of the bones may be from a hurricane in 1865. Elvira may be one of them. Or she may be the daughter of one of the building's previous owners. Wherever they came from, all are said to haunt Captain Tony's to this day.

MOST HOLY TRINITY CHURCH BROOKLYN, NEW YORK

When the current Most Holy Trinity Church was built in the late 1800s, it included a school building. Unfortunately, this school was built on the site of an old cemetery. According to legend, all the bodies were to moved to new graves, but som were left behind. Their unhap spirits haunt the school. Light flicker on and off, and ghostly voices can be heard. No wonc people think it's a bad idea to build on top of a cemetery!

It's also said that a bell ringer who was murdered in the church still haunts the **belfry** He's responsible for ringing the bell when there's appare no one there.

LOOK AT THE EVIDENCE

Ghosts often get blamed when light flicker, or turn on and off, as they do Most Holy Trinity Church. But are th the only possible explanation? Man people think this particular occurre could be the result of something as simple as faulty wiring.

DOORWAY TO HELL

Ghosts are bad enough, but there are some places in the world that are said to be home to things that are even worse. One such place is a cemetery in the town of Stull, Kansas. Stories say that it holds a doorway to hell.

Demonic Church

The Stull Cemetery has long been the subject of spooky legends. One involves an old tree that was supposedly used to hang witches. Other stories involve a now ruined church at the center of the cemetery. It was said bottles wouldn't break against its walls. As well, even after the roof was gone, rain would not fall inside the church. All this has led to Stull Cemetery being considered one of the most evil places on Earth. They're the kind of rumors that make an amazing story. But are they true?

DID YOU KNOW?

Although there have long been eerie rumors about the cemetery, most of them weren't very well known until 1974. That's when a local college newspaper published an article that popularized many of the stories. From there, the legend grew and became wilder with every telling.

*According to legend, evil came to Stull Cemetery when witches were hanged on a tree there. A stairway opened to the underworld, but it is well hidden. On top of that, the stairway can be used only at the spring **equinox** and Halloween. Do you think any of this legend could be true?*

No Trespassing!

The cemetery became so popular that visitors, especially on Halloween night, began numbering in the hundreds. It got so bad that the local sheriff's department had to post deputies there on Halloween night. Today, trespassers can be given a hefty fine for exploring the cemetery. They might even face jail time!

As a result, investigators have had a difficult time figuring how much of Stull's reputation is fact and how much is fiction. None of the many ghost-hunting TV shows have ever been given permission to enter the cemetery's gates. It's understandable that the town wants to protect itself and its reputation from people who might do harm. At the same time, this protectiveness has led many to believe that the town must be hiding something.

SALEM CEMETERY

Salem Cemetery, located in Hendrysburg, Ohio, is apparently home to the ghost of Louiza Catherine Fox. She was the first person murdered in nearby Kirkwood Township. She was killed by her fiancé in 1869 when her parents broke off their engagement. Today, visitors to the cemetery say you can see her ghost crying at her grave. These visitors have also taken to leaving gifts at her grave, but they have not seemed to help ease her sorrow.

LOOK AT THE EVIDENCE

With the restrictions placed on visitors to Stull Cemetery, it's hard to confirm or deny any of the **sinister** stories about it. However, the fact that many of these stories can be traced to a single article from 1974 seems somewhat suspicious. Is it possible that most of the crazy legends were just the product of a college student's overactive imagination?

BRUTAL GHOST OF SIR GEORGE MACKENZIE

The Greyfriars **Kirkyard** in Edinburgh, Scotland, dates all the way back to the 1500s. It gets its name from an old **monastery** that used to stand there. The monks who called it home wore gray robes. The cemetery itself was established in 1561.

Brutal Prison

Greyfriars Kirkyard also played an important part in Scottish history. In 1638, a document called the National Covenant was signed by a large number of Covenanters. Covenanters were members of a Presbyterian group who objected to changes in their traditional religion. Eventually, they were defeated by English forces. About 1,200 Covenanters were imprisoned in and around Greyfriars. They were treated so cruelly that only 257 made it out alive.

The cemetery surrounds Greyfriars Church, which has a history of fires and accidents. Could there be a paranormal connection?

Greyfriars is a fascinating and beautiful place by day, but many people avoid it at night.

Tomb of "Bluidy" Mackenzie

One of the main opponents of the Covenanters was a man named Sir George "Bluidy" (Bloody) Mackenzie. Bluidy Mackenzie loved to see the Greyfriars prisoners suffer tortures and hardships. When Mackenzie eventually died, he was laid to rest in the Greyfriars Kirkyard, in a large tomb.

Apparently, death has done nothing to curb his more unpleasant traits. In 1999, a homeless man managed to make his way into Mackenzie's tomb to try and escape the brutal Scottish winter. Apparently he tried to sleep IN Mackenzie's coffin, but when he climbed inside, it crumbled around him. The poor man ran terrified into the freezing night, crying that he had awakened Mackenzie's ghost.

HIGHGATE CEMETERY, LONDON

Many famous people have been buried in Highgate Cemetery in London, England, since it opened in 1839. Its most famous resident, however, may be the Highgate Vampire. This tall, shadowy figure was first reported in the 1960s. One legend says he is a Romanian vampire, like Dracula, from the 1500s who ended up buried there. Many vampire hunters have tried to prove that he exists. All have failed, but people in the area are still wary of Highgate.

Mackenzie's tomb is kept locked because of many attacks by vandals.

Ghosts on a Rampage

Since then, Mackenzie's ghost has been on a violent rampage. More than 150 visitors to the cemetery have passed out cold. There have also been over 400 documented injuries to people who have gone to the prison area or the cemetery. These include burns, bruises, and scratches. A few unlucky folks even said they had bones broken!

Many people blame the Mackenzie **poltergeist** for the injuries. Others say the spirits of his victims might share the blame. After all, if you went through what Mackenzie's prisoners did in life, you'd probably be pretty ticked about it, too!

DID MACKENZIE'S GHOST KILL THE MINISTER?

Colin Grant was a minister and a spirit medium. In 1999, he tried to exorcise, or drive out, the specters in Greyfriars—but instead he was driven away. Grant said he could not overcome all the evil. In fact, he feared for his life. A few months later, Grant died of a sudden heart attack. Some people said Mackenzie's angry spirit had reached out and killed him.

All the ghost tales have made the Greyfriars Kirkyard seem scarier over the years. Some visitors become hysterical and have to leave.

20

Would You Dare?

If you're ever in Greyfriars Kirkyard, and you're feeling especially brave, there's a nursery rhyme that is said to enrage old Bluidy Mackenzie. Here it is: "Bluidy Mackenzie, come oot if ye daur, lift the sneck and draw the bar!" Of course, if you recite it and find yourself leaving bruised and bloody, you have nobody to blame but yourself!

GREYFRIARS BOBBY

Greyfriars Kirkyard is not all gloom and doom. Since 1873, a statue of Greyfriars Bobby, an adorable Skye terrier, has stood opposite the entrance to the graveyard. The story goes that Bobby's owner died and was buried in Greyfriars Kirkyard. Bobby arrived shortly afterward. He spent the rest of his life, 14 years, watching over his master's final resting place. When Bobby died, he was buried nearby. People say his ghost still keeps watch over his owner.

LOOK AT THE EVIDENCE

The high number of injuries people receive at Greyfriars Kirkyard certainly seems incredible. However, another phenomenon might be easier to explain. The reason so many people faint might be as simple as stress. Think about it. You find yourself at night, in a creepy graveyard, where you're told HUNDREDS of people have actually been injured. In a situation like that, it's not crazy to think that a person might pass out from sheer nervousness or fear.

BONE-CHILLING CRYPTS
AND CATACOMBS

Completed in 1631, the Santa Maria della Concezione dei Cappuccini has stood in Rome for almost 400 years. It was built to house an order of monks known as Capuchins. When the monks first moved in, they brought the remains of thousands of their deceased brothers with them. These remains were then used to decorate the walls of the new **crypt** under the church. Imposing designs made of human bones and skulls are both beautiful and disturbing at the same time.

Historians say the crypt holds the remains of about 4,000 monks. Some skeletons still wear their hooded monk's habit.

Ghastly Remains

The crypt has a number of spooky features, including an entire area just for pelvic bones. Also, with the invention of electric light, some remains were turned into something like a lamp! The church says that these displays are not meant to be scary. They were put there to remind us that everyone dies eventually.

Resting in Peace

When you hear about an elaborate underground crypt decorated with skeletons, you might think it must be ULTRA haunted. Surprisingly, you'd be wrong. The crypt at Santa Maria is a peaceful place. A little freaky, sure, but there are no reports of ghostly disturbances or hauntings. It just goes to show, sometimes the places that seem the most likely to be haunted, aren't. You can never quite be sure with ghosts!

CATACOMBS OF PARIS

Of course, sometimes people see ghosts right where you would expect them. Take the **catacombs** beneath the city of Paris, France. Starting in 1786, remains were moved from cemeteries around the city to underground tunnels. Today, the catacombs hold the remains of over six million people. Skulls and other bones line the walls in elaborate patterns. It's said the ghost of a man named Philibert Aspairt haunts the catacombs. In 1793, he ventured into the catacombs, possibly to steal wine, but became lost. His bones were found 11 years later. People say his ghost returns every November to cause mischief in the tunnels.

DID YOU KNOW?

A plaque in the crypt speaks for the bones. It tells visitors: "What you are now, we once were; what we are now, you shall be." This now-famous saying is posted in three languages.

INDIA'S MOST HAUNTED CEMETERY

The South Park Street Cemetery in Kolkata, India, is one of the oldest cemeteries on the planet that isn't connected to a church. It was also once one of the largest Christian cemeteries outside England and America. The cemetery was used until around 1830. Today, it is a protected **heritage** site. It's home to a number of beautiful tombs. These structures are in a number of architectural styles. Some have a castle-like European style with tall spires. Others have a more traditional Indian look.

Wild trees and plants grow in many parts of the cemetery. The greenery keeps it cool and damp in Kolkata's daytime heat.

Visitors in Distress

While the cemetery might seem like a good place for a relaxing walk, some visitors have reported a less than pleasant visit. People have felt dizzy or ill while there. Some visitors say they have photographed weird structures that weren't visible to the naked eye. Other people have even claimed they had a hard time breathing, despite the fact they don't normally have any such issues. However, many visitors report witnessing nothing unusual. What could be responsible for such different experiences?

SPOOKY PLACE

The South Park Street Cemetery opened in 176 It was a graveyard for pe from Britain and other European countries who had moved to India. Son these people found succ but many died young of diseases that swept thro Kolkata. The cemetery was built with high wal in an attempt to stop th terrifying diseases from spreading. Funerals we usually held at night, w friends and family carr the coffin in an eerie torchlight procession.

People soon began to that many of the tomb were haunted, especia by people whose lives cut short. One is calle bleeding tomb" becau sometimes oozes a bl like substance. It's the resting place of a fam who died tragically w weeks of one anothe

LOOK AT THE EVIDENCE

There are a few reasons people might have hugely different experiences at the South Park Street Cemetery. Believers in the supernatural might claim that people who feel something there are more sensitive or open to paranormal phenomena. Skeptics might claim that there's an environmental factor. For example, pollution might make someone feel dizzy or sick, or make it difficult to breathe. What do you think?

ANCIENT GHOSTS OF THE VALLEY OF THE KINGS

In Egypt, one can find some of the most famous tombs ever made. Ancient Egyptians believed that you could take things with you from your time on Earth to the afterlife. As a result, many of their rulers, or pharaohs, built huge, elaborate final resting places. They then filled them with things they believed they might need. These included riches and jewels, food and wine, and even **mummified** pets. They were also buried with ushabti, small statues that were intended to work as servants in the afterlife. The process of mummification came about because of these beliefs. Egyptians thought you took your physical body with you, so it was preserved to last for as long as possible!

Some of the tombs, including King Tut's (see page 27), contain shrines to the jackal-headed god Anubis. He was associated with death and funerals.

Disturbed Afterlife

The Valley of the Kings is an area in Egypt where many of these burial tombs have been found. Both treasure hunters and archaeologists have targeted them to see what secrets they hold. However, some people think that these invasions have disturbed the ancient rulers buried there. Many people have claimed to see a ghostly pharaoh riding in a chariot. Night watchmen have also reported hearing footsteps and screams. They believe these are the sounds of former kings looking for their stolen treasure. And there have long been stories about mummy's curses that spell doom for anyone foolish enough to enter a tomb.

The Valley of the Kings is located in the Theban Hills. More than 60 burial places have been found there.

THE PHARAOH'S CURSE

King Tutankhamun is one of the most famous pharaohs still remembered today. When his tomb was opened in 1922, it created a sensation. Some also believe it activated an ancient curse! Lord Carnarvon was a wealth British man who funded the excavation of Tut's tomb. Within a year, he was dead. Within 12 years, eight more people who were present when the tomb was opened followed him to their graves. While this sounds ominous, skeptics point out that there were 58 people there that day. In fact, the head of the expedition, Howard Carter, lived until 1939. If the curse was going to go after anyone, surely he'd have been higher on the list!

Tut's gold death mask is now at a museum in Cairo. He was only a teen—was he cursed?

WHAT DO YOU THINK?

Graveyards and nearby churches are considered eerie places in many cultures because funerals and burials are held there. People think that if any place was going to be haunted, it would be a cemetery.

But not all cultures fear the dead. Mexico's Day of the Dead, for example, is a festive event. The Torajan peoples of Indonesia do even more to celebrate their dead. They hold elaborate funerals that can last for weeks. A body may be kept at home and treated like a living family member until the funeral. Then they lay their dead to rest in caves, stone graves, or hanging coffins where they can be easily reached. Every August, they take out the bodies, clean them, and dress them up. Then they all attend a festival called Ma'nene.

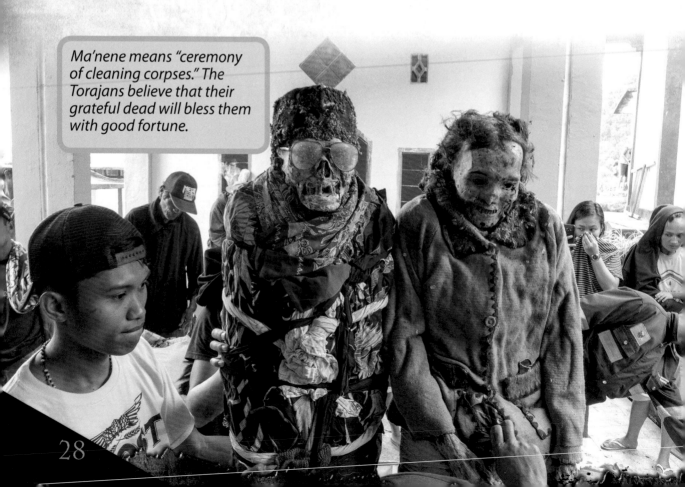

Ma'nene means "ceremony of cleaning corpses." The Torajans believe that their grateful dead will bless them with good fortune.

Fun or Gain?

Even if a ghost story isn't true, it can still teach you things. Many ghost stories have a basis in local history. These tales can be a fun way to learn about where you're from, or a place you're visiting. It's also fun to think about why people tell these kinds of stories, and why we've been telling them for so long. Are they just meant to thrill? What other reason might people have for telling ghost stories? When someone tells you that a place is haunted, it's important to use critical thinking. Why is this person telling you the story? Think about the situation. Are you gathered around a campfire, trying to out-scare each other? Or is the person asking for money to "prove" the ghost exists?

A 1928 photo shows Helen Duncan in a **séance** with a fake ghost.

FAMOUS HOAXES

HELEN DUNCAN - THE GHOST FABRICATOR

Helen Duncan was both a famous Scottish medium and a famous fraud. Duncan, who was born in 1897, was fascinated by the paranormal as a child. When she grew up, she made her living by holding séances in darkened rooms. She would spew what she called "ectoplasm" from her mouth. She said spirits materialized from the stringy white goo and communicated with their loved ones. Duncan's clients believed in her even after a series of photos were taken in 1928. These photos showed that a "spirit" was a paper-mache doll wrapped in a sheet.

Duncan's tricks were exposed again and again. She was arrested in 1944 during a séance. Her "ectoplasm" was made from cheesecloth or paper and egg whites that she would swallow before a séance. She was convicted of fake witchcraft under a 200-year-old law and spent nine months in jail. Yet many people still believed in her. By 1951, the witchcraft law had been repealed. Duncan died in 1956, but her followers are still trying to get an official pardon for her!

BOOKS

Ancient Egypt: Tales of Gods and Pharaohs by Marcia Williams, Candlewick, 2013.

Ghostly Graveyards by Judy Allen, Bearport Publishing, 2016.

Greyfriars Bobby: A Tale of Victorian Edinburgh by Frances and Gordon Jarvie, NMSE - Publishing, 2010.

The Roman Catacombs by Enzo George, Gareth Stevens Publishing, 2017.

Spooky Cemeteries by Dinah Williams, Bearport Publishing, 2008.

St. Louis Cemetery No. 1 by Michael Ferut, Torque, 2014.

WEBSITES

More information about cemeteries in New Orleans
www.saveourcemeteries.org/

More information about the curse of Tutankhamun's tomb
http://ancientegyptonline.co.uk/tutcurse.html

More information about the Paris catacombs
www.catacombes.paris.fr/en/catacombs

Key West's Most Haunted

https://hauntedkeywest.com/2014/02/12/key-wests-most-haunted-top-10/

GLOSSARY

afterlife The place some people believe we go to when we die

apparitions Ghosts

belfry A bell tower, especially one that is part of a church

catacombs An underground cemetery with rooms in which to bury human remains

cathedral A church that contains the seat of a bishop, a high-ranking priest. This makes it the central church for its area.

crypt An underground room beneath a church used as a burial place

earthwork A large, human-made pile of soil, often made as a defense

equinox Either of the two times each year (March 21 and September 23) when day and night are of same length

fraud A person who is not what he or she pretends to be

heritage Something important to an area's culture or history

kirkyard A churchyard, often used as a burial ground

monastery A type of religious building where monks and nuns live

mortal Relating to, or connected with, death

mummified Preserved by being embalmed and wrapped in cloth

pagan A person who believes in many gods

paranormal See supernatural

phenomena Rare or important events, often without a clear cause

plague A contagious disease that is caused by bacteria, spreads quickly, and can kill many people

poltergeist An unseen spirit that causes physical disturbances

possessed Controlled by an evil spirit

séance A meeting at which people try to make contact with the dead

sinister Evil or bad

specters Ghosts or spirits

supernatural Something out of the ordinary that seemingly cannot be explained by science

voodoo Religion from Africa that includes the connection to ancestral spirits and the practice of magic

widow A woman whose spouse has died

31

INDEX